The Jesus Jokebook

The Jesus Jokebook

Des MacHale

MERCIER PRESS

WHAT YOU NEED TO READ

MERCIER PRESS
Douglas Village, Cork
www.mercierpress.ie

Trade enquiries to Columba Mercier Distribution,
55a Spruce Avenue, Stillorgan Industrial Park,
Blackrock, Co. Dublin

ISBN: 978 1 85635 562 9

10 9 8 7 6 5 4 3 2 1

 Mercier Press receives financial assist-
ance from the Arts Council/An Chomhairle
Ealaíon

Printed and bound by J.H. Haynes & Co. Ltd, Sparkford

Introduction

It was with some trepidation that I decided to write *The Jesus Jokebook*. I am, and have been as long as I can remember, a practising Catholic and I take my religion very seriously. I firmly believe that Jesus Christ was true man and true God and that He died to save me. There is always the strong possibility that I will be struck down by a thunderbolt if I have crossed over the lines of blasphemy and good taste. But as one musical commentator has said, 'Why should the devil have all the good tunes?' Hymns of praise to God can be beautiful and melodious too. I feel somewhat the same about jokes and humour – why should the devil have all the laughs? Why shouldn't believers laugh too?

Jesus was fully human and like all human beings must have had a keen sense of humour – in fact with the task He set himself of redeeming mankind, He probably needed a colossal sense of humour. I have scoured the gospels and found what I believe to be many instances of humour, irony and even jokes in those sacred pages. Jesus was a joyful person and must have laughed a great deal, though not much of His laughter was recorded. G.K. Chesterton has suggested that, His sense of humour was so great that He did not dare to show it to us in case we would not take His message seriously. That is a very pleasant thought that Christian prophets of doom and killjoys might like to take on board. There is a much better chance of finding laughter in Heaven than in Hell.

I will admit that in the course of my researches I did come across many blasphemous and obscene jokes involving Jesus and I certainly have not included them in this collection. Actually, I found none of these particularly funny and they taught me nothing about either Jesus or humour. The jokes I have included are, I hope, funny and not offensive to believers. Christians, unlike some other religions, have a long and healthy tradition of laughing at themselves.

Viewed from the right point of view, each of these jokes has a message – almost a mini-sermon which can teach us something about this remarkable man. I firmly believe that not only are humour and religious belief not incompatible, but that they can actually improve and complement each other. To preachers and pastors I say, use these jokes freely in your dealings with your flock and let them leave the church with a smile on their faces – but always be sensitive to people's beliefs.

Like most Irishmen, I am banking very heavily on the assumption that Jesus has a strong sense of humour. Otherwise, forgive me my trespasses!

DES MACHALE

SALVA REVERENTIA

*I*t was the morning after the wedding feast of Cana and Joseph had drunk a little too freely of the excellent wine. He had a terrible hangover and as he lay in his bed he called down to his wife in the kitchen, 'Mary, please send me up a glass of water, and for God's sake keep the child away from it this time.'

Jesus was showing a group of newcomers around Heaven – all the mansions in his Father's house. They came across one huge enclosure with high walls.

'What is that building called?' one of the newcomers asked.

'Ssh,' said Jesus, 'that's where we house all the Catholics. They think they're the only ones here.'

A rabbi and a priest were arguing about Jesus' race and who should be allowed to claim him.

'Jesus was definitely Jewish,' insisted the rabbi.

'But only on His mother's side,' said the priest.

Jesus would never have been promoted in the university system. He was a terrific teacher but He never published anything.

Jesus was walking around Heaven making sure that everyone was blissfully happy when He came across an old man sitting in the corner weeping bitterly.

'Come along,' said Jesus, 'we can't have this, you're supposed to be happy here.'

'I'll never be happy here,' said the man, 'when I was on earth I was a carpenter and one day my son left and I never saw him again.'

'Daddy?' said Jesus.

'Pinocchio,' said the man.

A Jewish man complained to the police that he had been beaten up by two Irishmen.

When questioned, the Irishmen said that they had done it because the Jewish people had crucified Jesus.

'But that was over two thousand years ago,' said the bewildered policeman.

'Well *we* only heard about it last night,' said the Irishmen.

A lot of women feel that Jesus was like most typical men.

They say they will come back but then you never see them again.

Why does God the Father write with His left hand?

Because Jesus is sitting on His right hand.

11

There was a big born-again meeting in a large hall in Belfast and a former lady sinner was on stage with a microphone in her hand recounting her experiences.

'Last night,' she told the congregation, 'I was in the arms of Satan, but tonight I am in the arms of Jesus.'

A voice from the back of the hall boomed out, 'How are you fixed for tomorrow night?'

A Scotsman was on a visit to the Holy Land and took a trip to the Sea of Galilee where Jesus walked on water.

'How much for a return boat trip across the lake?' he asked the boatman.

'Fifty dollars,' he was told.

'That's a Hell of a fare,' said the Scotsman, 'no wonder Jesus walked.'

Why did Mary and Joseph take Jesus with them to Jerusalem?

Babysitters were hard to get even in those days.

It was Easter morning and Jesus was rising from the dead. He rolled back the stone but was very annoyed to find nobody there to greet Him. So He stormed down town but there was nobody about. Then He heard the sound of music, singing and carousing coming from an upper room, so He knocked on the door. Out came Peter and said: 'Oh Jesus, I'm sorry; we completely forgot you were rising from the dead this morning. You know what it's like when Judas gets a few bob.'

'Where does Jesus live?' a little girl was asked by her teacher.

'He lives in our bathroom miss,' replied the little girl.

'What on earth makes you think that?' said the horrified teacher.

'Well,' said the little girl, 'every morning my dad shouts, 'Jesus, are you still in there?'

It was the annual Heaven versus Hell football match with Jesus managing Heaven and Satan managing Hell.

'I'm very confident of victory,' said Jesus to the TV interviewer. 'After all, we have all the best players up here – Best, Matthews, Bobby Moore and lots of others.'

'How do you feel about the match Nick?' Satan was asked.

'Put your money on Hell,' said the Devil, 'after all, we have all the referees.'

When Jesus was born He weighed exactly seven pounds. How do we know?

He had a weigh in a manger.

A Mafia chief's little boy wanted a bicycle so his father said he should pray to Jesus for one. So the little boy prayed and prayed and prayed but no bicycle was forthcoming.

So one night he crept into a church with a plastic bag and put the statue of the Virgin Mary into the bag. And he left a note for Jesus which read:

'If you ever want to see your mother again, give me that bicycle now.'

Classic graffiti seen in Liverpool:

WHAT WILL WE DO WHEN JESUS COMES TO LIVERPOOL?

MOVE ST. JOHN TO CENTRE FORWARD.

Cecil B. de Mille arrived at the gates of Heaven but was refused entry by Saint Peter.

'Let me talk to Jesus,' says de Mille, so Jesus is sent for.

'I agree with Saint Peter,' says Jesus, 'we cannot let you in.'

'Look,' said de Mille, 'I made you – I can break you.'

A priest and a rabbi were talking on a train.

'What are the promotion prospects like in your church?' the rabbi asked.

'Pretty good,' said the priest, 'I could be made a parish priest.'

'And then?'

'A monsignor.'

'And then?'

'A bishop.'

'And then?'

'A cardinal.'

'And then?'

'Pope.'

'And then?'

'There's nothing higher than Pope,' said the priest, 'except God.'

'One of our boys made it,' said the rabbi.

Graffiti spotted in Jerusalem:

CANCEL EASTER – THEY'VE FOUND THE BODY

This little Jewish boy wasn't doing very well at mathematics in school so his parents moved him to a state school. He didn't do very well there either so they moved him to a Church of England school. It was the same story there so finally they moved him to a Catholic school. To their amazement he came top of the class in mathematics with 100 per cent in every exam.

Intrigued, they asked him to explain.

17

'Well,' he told them, 'they take maths very seriously in that school. They've got a fellow nailed to the plus sign.'

What were the last words of Jesus on the cross?

What a way to spend Easter!

A liberal theologian's explanation – Judas needed the money for a sick friend.

A little boy was writing an essay on the visit of the three Wise Men to Bethlehem.

Part of it read: And they brought the baby Jesus gifts of gold, Frankenstein and myrrh.

Jesus saw the deaf man and He took pity on

him and restored his hearing. And Jesus saw the blind man and he took pity on him and restored his sight. And Jesus saw the crippled man and took pity on him but the crippled man shouted, 'Don't touch me, I've got a disability pension.'

Underneath a poster which read:

JESUS SAVES

Someone had written:

BUT MOSES INVESTS

Jesus was a lively little lad in His family home in Nazareth. He would run in the front door and not close it behind Him.

And Joseph would shout after Him, 'Hey, were you born in a stable or what?'

One of the three Wise Men was very tall so as he was going into the stable at Bethlehem he hit his head on the frame of the stable door.

'Jesus Christ,' he said in anger.

'That's a nice name,' said Mary. 'We were going to call Him Marvin, but I think we'll call Him that instead.'

A little boy was asked in bible class to draw a picture of Mary, Joseph and the baby Jesus on their flight into Egypt. He produced a picture of an airplane with four figures.

'What do these figures represent?' his teacher asked.

'Well, those three are Mary, Joseph and the baby Jesus,' he replied.

'And who is the fourth?'

'That's Pontius the Pilot.'

Graffiti scrawled under a poster which read:

WHERE WILL YOU BE WHEN JESUS COMES?

STILL HERE WAITING FOR A NUMBER 23 BUS!!

What is the difference between Jesus and a medical consultant?

Jesus doesn't think He's a medical consultant.

Why wasn't Jesus born in Dublin?

They couldn't find three Wise Men there – or a virgin.

The Pope was in the middle of an audience when a cardinal came and whispered in his ear, 'Jesus is on the phone and wants to have a word with you.'

So the Pope rushed away to his private chamber and returned a few minutes later to his pilgrims.

'I have good news and bad news for you,' he told them.

'That was Jesus on the phone and He has just arrived on earth for the second coming.

That was the good news. The bad news is that He was calling from Salt Lake City.'

The mob were about to stone a woman caught committing adultery when Jesus came along and began to write all their sins with a stick in the sand.

'Let those among you without sin cast the first stone,' he told them.

At this, a great big rock came flying through the crowd and hit Him on the back of the head.

Without turning around Jesus said, 'Mother, sometimes I hate you.'

Knock Knock.

Who's there?

Jesus.

Jesus who?

Ah, how quickly people forget.

God the Father, Saint Peter and Jesus arrive at the bank of a river where a large crowd of potential converts is waiting on the other side.

'If we want some new members,' said Saint Peter, 'we'd better perform a cool miracle.'

'I'll walk across the water,' says God the Father, and promptly sinks into the river.

'I'll give it a go,' says Saint Peter and promptly sinks as well.

Finally Jesus walks across the river to the cheers of the crowd.

'Just how did you do that miracle?' asks God the Father.

'What miracle?' said Jesus. 'I just used the stepping stones.'

The guards at the empty Easter tomb of Jesus were charged with incompetence by their Roman centurion.

'What did you expect?' asked one. 'Did you tell us we were supposed to be guarding the Son of God? NOOOOOOOOOO!'

Jesus, Mary, and Joseph were going about their daily work at their home in Nazareth when suddenly Jesus ran outside into Joseph's carpenter shop and said, 'Did you call me?'

'No,' said Joseph, 'I just hit my thumb with the hammer again.'

One day Jesus was looking down on the world

and despairing about human behaviour. So He sent down a host of angels to take a survey and find out what percentage of humanity was leading a good life and what percentage was leading an evil life.

Within a short time the news came back: 5 per cent good, 95 per cent evil.

Very upset, Jesus nevertheless decided to send an encouraging e-mail to the good 5 per cent to keep them going and to urge them not to despair.

Do you know what that email said?

No?

So you didn't get one either?

A little boy was asked by his religion teacher how he would recognise Jesus if He came back again today.

'Easy,' said the little boy, 'He wears His heart outside His chest.'

A fellow was behaving suspiciously near the gates of Heaven. First he approached the gates then walked away, then he approached the gates and went back again. When he had done this for the third time, Saint Peter called for Jesus who decided to confront the man.

'Look, what are you playing at?' Jesus asked.

'Well,' said the man, 'you know I'm dead, I know I'm dead – now if somebody would just tell the cardiac resuscitation team ...'

A rabbi was worried that his son was about to convert to Christianity so he prayed fervently to God to prevent this from happening.

'My son wants to become a Christian, please stop him O God,' he prayed.

The voice of God boomed back.

'What can I do? Look at my own son ...'

Why is Jesus so popular in Ireland?

He was the first man to turn water into wine.

Bill Gates prayed to Jesus to become the richest man in the world. Jesus answered his prayer but told him there would be one condition. For the rest of his life he would look like a turtle.

One of the greatest acts of forgiveness in the Gospels is that Peter became one of the disciples despite the fact that Jesus had healed his mother-in-law.

The Pope and a cardinal were sitting in the

Vatican drinking coffee when a young priest ran in and said Jesus was visiting Earth and heading their way. The Pope headed for his typewriter and began writing a new encyclical.

'What do I do?' asked the cardinal.

'Look busy,' said the Pope.

A religion teacher was teaching a class about Jesus' parable of the Good Samaritan. He was worried that the children might misunderstand the part where it said that a priest passed the wounded man by and thought he had better explain that the priest was on his way to the temple and would be defiled if he touched the man's body.

'Why do you think the priest passed the man by?' he asked the class.

One little fellow raised his hand.

'What's the reason Tommy?' asked the teacher.

'Because he saw the man had already been robbed,' said the little fellow.

A burglar broke into a house one night and was stumbling around in the dark when he heard a voice saying, 'Jesus will punish you.' Thinking he was just hearing things he continued, but again the voice rang out, 'Jesus will punish you.' So he switched on his torch and saw the voice was coming from a parrot.

'What is your name?' he asked the parrot.

'Moses,' the parrot replied.

The burglar laughed and said, 'What kind of people would call their parrot Moses?'

The parrot replied, 'The same kind of people who would call their pitbull Jesus.'

Moses, God the Father and Jesus were playing golf together. Moses drove off on the first par three and the ball landed three feet from the hole. Then Jesus drove off and the ball landed two feet from the hole. God the Father then hit off, but topped His drive and so it landed just a few yards off the tee in the rough. Suddenly a rabbit emerged from his burrow and took the ball in his mouth and began to run towards the clubhouse. An eagle swooped from the air, grabbed the rabbit with the ball still in his mouth and flew down the fairway. Over the green he was attacked by another eagle so he dropped the rabbit who dropped the ball straight into the hole.

Jesus turned and said, 'Come on, Dad, it's only a game.'

'Typical,' Mary the mother of Jesus was heard to say, 'you wait ages for a wise man and then three come along together.'

An American soldier came across the following message scribbled on a wall in Iraq:

NO JESUS IN IRAQ

Underneath he wrote:

LUCKY OLD JESUS

Why is it a good job that Jesus was crucified and not electrocuted?

Because a billion Catholics bless themselves with the sign of the cross instead of going aaarrrggghhh and convulsing.

Little Mister Cohen had his clothes shop in a difficult location. On his left hand side was a huge department store owned by a Catholic and on his right hand side was an equally big store owned by a Protestant. When Easter came both the Catholic and Protestant shopowners displayed a huge sign which read:

They urged Cohen to do the same so he displayed a huge sign which read:

JESUS IS RISEN, BUT COHEN'S PRICES REMAIN THE
SAME

Sign seen on a southern evangelist church:

JESUS LOVES ALL DENOMINATIONS
BUT HIS FAVOURITE IS THE $100 BILL

At the last supper Jesus stands up and announces that he is going to turn the water into wine.

'No you won't,' shouts Judas. 'Put in your hundred shekels like everyone else.'

And Jesus said to the theologians, 'Who do you say that I am?'

And they replied, 'You are the eschatological manifestation of the ground of our being, the charisma from which we derive the ultimate meaning in all of our interpersonal relationships.'

And Jesus said 'What?'

Even at the age of four, a young boy was stage struck and wanted to be a great actor. He was therefore very annoyed not to be given the top part of Joseph in the school nativity play but was cast as the innkeeper instead. On the night of the performance he gained his revenge. When Mary and Joseph arrived at the inn he greeted them saying, 'Come on in, we have a room reserved for you.'

At Sunday school each of the children was

asked to put their penny in the collection box and at the same time quote an appropriate verse spoken by Jesus in the Gospels.

The first little girl put in her penny saying, 'It is more blessed to give than to receive.'

The second child said, 'The Lord loves a cheerful giver.'

The final little fellow reluctantly put in his penny saying, 'The fool and his money are soon parted.'

Two chancers were sacked from their jobs and received their redundancy money. They decided to set up a painting and decorating firm and offered to paint the local church for €1,000. But long before the job was finished they ran out of paint so they bought several cans of turpentine and diluted what little paint they had left to finish the job.

A few weeks later they returned to the church and found the paint blistered and cracked because they had diluted it too much.

As they tried to sneak out of the church the voice of Jesus rang out, 'Repaint you thinners!'

A priest was driving along on his motorbike at over seventy kilometres an hour when he was stopped by a policeman.

'You were going too fast for someone with L plates father; if it was anyone else I'd be inclined to book you.'

'Don't worry my son,' said the priest, 'Jesus is with me.'

'In that case,' said the policeman, 'I'm definitely going to book you. You're not allowed to carry a passenger.'

An Irish Catholic priest, an English Anglican vicar and a Scottish Presbyterian minister were discussing what proportion of their weekly collection went to Jesus.

The priest said, 'I draw a line on the floor and throw all the money up in the air. What falls on the left side I keep and what falls on the right side goes to Jesus.'

The vicar said, 'I draw a circle on the ground and throw all the money up in the air. What falls inside the circle I keep and what falls outside goes to Jesus.'

The minister said, 'I throw all the money up in the air and what Jesus doesn't want He sends back down again.'

It's a good job that the disciples Jesus called were fishermen and not cabinet makers. Otherwise he would have had to say to them: 'Drop your drawers and follow me.'

After the resurrection Jesus tried to walk on water again. But he forgot about the holes in his feet.

Paddy, an old Irish Catholic, was on his death-bed. But thank God he wasn't dying of anything serious.

On one side of his bed was his faithful old doctor who gave him a bill for €1,000.

On the other side of his bed was his old friend the parish priest who suggested that Paddy hand over €1,000 for masses for the immortal repose of his soul.

'How are you feeling?' Paddy's wife asked him.

'Happy,' smiled Paddy, 'I feel like Jesus – dying between two thieves.'

Two four-year-old kids were discussing theology as four-year-old kids do.

'What do you think of all this Jesus business?' one asked the other, 'Does Jesus exist?'

'Of course He does,' replied the other, 'who do you think opens the doors in supermarkets?'

A mother gave her two boys an apple each, one big and one small. One boy grabbed the big apple and gave the small one to his brother.

'Come, come,' said his mother, 'if you were Jesus, you'd have taken the small apple and given the big one to your brother.'

'OK,' said the lad with the big apple looking at his brother, 'you can be Jesus.'

A nun who was also a nurse in a hospital was taking down a patient's details. One patient gave his name and age but said he had no next of kin.

'Come on now,' she said to him, 'you must have some relative we can contact.'

'Well there is my sister, but she'd be no use because she's only a nun.'

'Only a nun? How dare you. I'll have you know she's the bride of Jesus.'

'In that case,' smiled the man, 'send all my medical bills to my brother-in-law.'

If the Holy family came back to Earth today, Joseph would publish a book about carpentry, Mary would do shampoo commercials and Jesus would be asked to perform His latest miracles on television.

QUOTES ABOUT JESUS

He is such a devout Catholic, he won't be satisfied until he is crucified like Jesus.

John B. Keane

I heard that Glenn Hoddle has found Jesus. That must have been one Hell of a pass.

Bob Davies

If English was good enough for Jesus, it's good enough for me.

David Edwards

I once said to a street evangelist, 'You mean Jesus is coming and you're dressed like that?'

Dave Barry

Remember, Jesus loves you – well someone has to.

John O'Connor

I want to play the role of Jesus. I'm a logical choice. I'm a Jew and a comedian. And I'm an atheist, so I'd be able to look at the character objectively.

Charlie Chaplin

It's just as well Jesus isn't around now. They would never have crucified Him – just given Him a hundred hours community service and that would have wrecked the Redemption.

Derek Nimmo

In the town of Athlone there was a young fellow with the unlikely name of Jesus Moloney. He loved to sing but, truth to tell, he had no voice at all and he made crows sound melodious. He was an enthusiastic member of the local church choir who tolerated his presence because of all the work he did.

One year the choir was invited to Rome to sing before the Pope and the question arose as to what to do with Jesus Moloney. It would break his heart to leave him behind but on the other hand his voice would give the Pope a nervous breakdown. So a compromise was reached – he would be part of the choir but would merely mime the words in front of the Pope. Came the big day and the performance went very well, but at the reception afterwards, the Pope, who had a keen ear for music and a sharp eye for detail, said to the choirmaster.

'Very nice, very nice, but I couldn't help noticing there was one young man in your choir, who didn't make any sound at all but just moved his lips in time with the others.'

'Jesus Moloney can't sing,' said the choir-master.

'Well Christ, couldn't he have tried at least,' said the Pope.

A well-known surgeon, and a confirmed atheist to boot (though he did worship the God Mammon), was about to perform a very difficult operation in a hospital owned by a religious order. Before the operation began one of his assistants, a nun, prayed loudly 'Jesus, Mary and Joseph help us.'

The surgeon replied curtly, 'Thank you sister, but I do not need any help from unqualified assistants.'

Three theologians were having a profound discussion as to whether God had a sense of humour or not.

'God has no sense of humour,' said the first, 'because humour demands incongruity and with God nothing is incongruous.'

'But Jesus was fully God and fully man,' said the second, 'and since all men have a sense of humour, He must have had a sense of humour.'

'The Holy Ghost is pure spirit,' said the third, 'and pure spirits cannot have a sense of humour.'

The theologians then had to write up an agreed report on their deliberations to submit to their bishop. Their statement read:

Every time a joke is told in Heaven, the second person of the Blessed Trinity has to explain it to the other two divine persons.

Some members of Catholic religious orders were arguing about what order Jesus would have belonged to if He were on earth now.

'He would be a Dominican,' said the first, 'because of His great preaching.'

'No, He would have been Franciscan,' said the second, 'because of His great humility.'

'Not at all, He would have been an Augustinian,' said the third, 'because of His great holiness.'

So they decided to pray to Jesus to send a signal from Heaven telling them the truth. And a little piece of paper floated down from the skies and it read:

Dear Friends,
Stop this squabbling at once.
Signed: Jesus SJ.

Jesus was once asked a trick question by the Pharisees.

'Can you make a stone so heavy even you cannot lift it?' he asked.

'Yes,' said Jesus, 'and then to prove I was God, I would lift it.'

This fellow, desperate for money, was in the habit of going into the church every day and praying before the statue of God to have the name of the winner of the upcoming Derby revealed to him. One day he had a few drinks on board and actually threatened God that he would damage His statue severely if the information was not forthcoming.

A priest in the church heard all this and replaced the statue of God with a smaller one of Jesus.

Next day the fellow came in and said, 'Did your father leave any message for me?'

Why did Jesus know the Old Testament so well?

Because His father wrote it.

'Please Jesus, send me a bicycle for my birthday,' a little boy prayed very loudly as he went to bed.

'There's no need to shout,' his mother told him, 'God isn't deaf.'

'I know that,' he said, 'but Grandma is.'

A terrorist arrived at the gates of Heaven only to be told by Jesus, 'You can't come in here because of your actions – go elsewhere.'

'I don't want to come in,' said the terrorist, 'but I wanted to let you know that you have five minutes to leave the building.'

A teenage son asked his father if he could borrow the family car for the evening.

'Certainly son,' said the father, 'on the condition that you get your hair cut.'

'But dad,' protests the son, 'Jesus wore his hair long.'

'Yes He did son,' smiled the father, 'but then Jesus walked everywhere too.'

A man visiting a psychiatric hospital was intrigued to hear a patient shouting, 'I'm Jesus, I'm Jesus, I'm Jesus!'

So he engaged him in conversation and asked him, 'How do you know you're Jesus?'

The man answered, 'I'm Jesus because God made me Jesus.'

'I did not,' came a voice from the corner.

A painter high up on scaffolding inside a big church saw a little old woman praying devoutly down below him, so he decided to have a little fun at her expense.

'Hello, this is Jesus speaking,' he said, but the lady did not react.

Again, louder, he said, 'Hello, this is Jesus speaking.' Again, there was no reaction.

Finally he shouted with all his might, 'Hello, this is Jesus speaking.'

Without lifting her head the old lady said, 'Be quiet, I'm speaking to your mother.'

A very rich man was dying and prayed and prayed and prayed to Jesus to be allowed to bring just one suitcase full of his worldly possessions with him to Heaven. Eventually the Heavenly authorities relented and said, 'OK – just one suitcase.' So the man filled a suitcase with gold bars and died happily. He was met at the pearly gates by Jesus himself who was checking that he wasn't trying to smuggle in any illegal substances. When He opened the suitcase He said, 'You could have brought anything you liked up here and you brought pavement?'

A little boy was being very naughty, so his

mother asked him how he expected to get to Heaven.

'Well,' he replied, 'I have a plan. When I get up to the gates, I'll run in and run out again. Then I'll run in and run out again. Then I'll run in and run out again.'

And then Jesus will shout, 'Look, are you going in or out?' and then I'll go in.'

There was a fixed race in the Bible. Jesus said to Lazarus, 'Come forth!' But Lazarus came fifth and a lot of money was lost.

M*RS MALAPROP ON JESUS*

Jesus was betrayed by Judas the carrycot.

Jesus was condemned by a bunch of spiders.

Jesus cured the ten leprechauns.

Jesus said, 'Blessed are the cheesemakers.'

Jesus had a lady friend called Mary Mandolin.

The baby Jesus was persecuted by King Horrid.

Instead of releasing Jesus they released Brer Rabbit.

They came to Jesus carrying a parable on a bed.

Jesus was followed everywhere by the twelve decibels.

In the olden days a priest bought a donkey to get from place to place. The man who sold the donkey told him that the animal responded to two simple commands – 'Amen' to stop and 'Praise Jesus' to start. This worked very well until one day the priest forgot the commands. The donkey was heading towards a steep cliff with the priest on his back – he tried every command he could think of to no avail and the donkey kept heading for the cliff edge. Finally he ended with the word 'Amen' so of course the donkey stopped a few inches from the cliff edge. 'Praise Jesus,' said the priest.

Why does Jesus not accept burnt offerings as a sacrifice?

Air pollution.

A little boy was attending Sunday school and was hearing for the first time about the cruel way in which Jesus had met His death by crucifixion.

'They would never have got away with it,' he hold his teacher, 'if Superman had been there.'

A little girl's pet cat died and her mother was trying to console her.

'Don't worry Shirley,' she said to her, 'little Fluffy is now in Heaven with Jesus.'

Shirley retorted, 'What would Jesus want with a dead cat?'

This fellow was desperately short of money so he prayed to Jesus every day to win the Lotto. Every day he prayed and prayed but there was no sign of a big win.

Finally he went into a church and prayed loudly, 'Jesus, what do I have to do to win the Lotto?'

And the voice of Jesus came booming back, 'Well for a start you could buy a ticket.'

A school allowed the children to write and produce their own nativity play unseen by the teachers until the opening night.

At the first performance the eight-year-old Joseph arrives home from work with his briefcase and is presented with his pipe and slippers and a kiss by his wife Mary.

'And how's our Jesus then?' he asks.

'Awful,' says Mary, 'He's been a right little bugger all day.'

This fellow was hanging by his fingernails from a cliff so he began to pray.

'Is there anybody up there?' he shouted.

'Yes my son,' said a voice, 'this is Jesus, how can I help you?'

'Save me Jesus,' said the fellow, 'don't let me perish.'

'Let go, my son,' said the voice, 'and I will catch you.'

There was silence for a few moments and the fellow said, 'Is there anybody else up there?'

A Belfast Protestant had just died and his widow was describing his last moments to her neighbour.

'First he asked for his wee fife, and then asked for his wee sash,' she told her.

'Finally, he asked for his wee drum, and shouting, 'To Hell with the Pope', he flew straight into the arms of Jesus.'

During the war, a father, mother and son were making their way home one night along a country road when they were stopped by a sentry.

'Halt, who goes there?' he shouted suddenly.

'Jesus, Mary and Joseph,' screamed the woman in fear.

'Pass, Holy family,' said the sentry.

A Welshman was marooned on a desert island for over fifteen years until finally he was rescued by a passing ship. When asked by the captain of the ship what had kept him going he replied that it was his faith in Jesus.

'Let me show you,' he said and took the captain to a clearing where he had built not one but two churches.

'But why two churches?' asked the captain. 'Surely one would have been enough?'

'Oh, that's the one I attend,' said the Welshman, 'and the other one is the one I don't go to.'

MORE QUOTES ABOUT JESUS

After washing twelve pairs of His disciples feet, the crucifixion must have been a pushover.

Alan Bennett

A survey has revealed that seventy per cent of Americans believe in Jesus and twenty per cent do not. Six per cent are not sure and four per cent believe they are Jesus.

James Adams

My father was not at all devout. But he saw Jesus as quite a good chap, as the honourable member for Galilee South.

Malcolm Muggeridge

If Jesus were alive today, there is definitely one thing He would not be – a Christian.

Mark Twain

The Lord will provide, but at the moment He is a little behind in His payments.

Spike Milligan

Short of showing Shakespeare round Stratford-upon-Avon, I would dearly love to show Jesus Christ round the Vatican.

Malcolm Muggeridge

During the last supper Jesus startled the apostles by announcing, 'One of you will betray me.'

Peter said, 'Surely not I, Lord?'

'I say unto you,' repeated Jesus, 'one of you will betray me.'

'Surely not I, Lord?' said Andrew.

'I say unto you verily,' said Jesus 'one of you here present will betray me.'

'Surely not I, Lord?' said Judas.

'Surely not I, Lord, surely not I, Lord,' Jesus mimicked him.

Look, I don't care whose star you are following, get that camel out of my garden.

FIRST REFERENCES IN THE BIBLE

TENNIS: And Jesus said, 'Let down thy net.' (Or Joseph was serving in the court of Pharaoh.)

AN IRISHMAN: And Jesus was teaching Daly in the temple.

MOTOR CARS: He came down the mountain in a Triumph and crossed the river in a Ford.

SUB AQUA: The Apostles spoke with divers' tongues.

POLE VAULTING: Jesus cleared the Temple.

A HATCHET: The axe of the Apostles.

CRICKET: Peter stood up with the eleven and was bold.

FOOTBALL: Jesus said, 'Beware of the leaven of the Pharisees.'

BOXING: Never fear, hit his eye.

A CRASH DIET: The angel Gabriel who came down to an ounce.

DRINK: He that is not with us is a Guinness.

Look, I don't care whose son you are, you can't walk on this lake while I'm fishing here.

Cancel Christmas – Joseph has confessed everything.

Jesus was disturbed by a loud knocking on the gates of Heaven.

'Who's there?' he asked.

'It is I,' came the reply.

'Go to Hell,' said Jesus, 'we have enough school teachers here already.'

This holy man arrived at the gates of Heaven and was very surprised to be greeted by the Devil, old Nick himself.

'Don't be alarmed,' said the Devil, 'we've gone comprehensive.'

This man was desperately ugly so he prayed to Jesus to send him some money for plastic surgery. Right enough he won a huge amount in the Lottery and had his plastic surgery but a few days later he died. While wandering around Heaven he met Jesus and asked Him, 'Why didn't you give me some time to enjoy my new good looks?'

'Sorry,' said Jesus, 'I just didn't recognise you.'

Murphy was an Irishman who had made a fortune in the hardware trade and his nails were famed throughout the land for their hardness and durability. So he decided to go international and launch a massive TV advertising campaign. He handed a million euro over to a PR company and said, 'You're the professionals – launch a TV advertising campaign that will popularise my nails all over the world.'

So one night he is watching TV with his family when his ad comes on. It shows Jesus on the cross and the voice-over says, 'For a really thorough job, use Murphy's nails.'

'Oh my God,' said Murphy, 'I'm ruined. I'll lose the custom of every God-fearing client I have.'

So he gets on the phone and says furiously to the PR rep, 'I want that ad taken off at once. Replace it with something less controversial or I'm not paying a single cent more.'

A few weeks later he is watching TV again when the new ad comes on. This time it shows Jesus triumphantly rising from the tomb and the voice-over saying, 'This would never have happened if they'd used Murphy's nails.'

How is it that when we talk to Jesus, we're praying, but when Jesus talks to us, we're schizophrenic?

A man was hanging by his fingernails over a sea cliff so he prayed to Jesus to save him.

'I will save you my son,' said the voice of Jesus, 'just have faith.'

Just then a boat came by and the sailor shouted, 'Jump, we will fish you from the water.'

'No,' said the man, 'Jesus is going to save me.'

A few minutes later a submarine surfaced but the man shouted, 'Go away, Jesus is going to save me.'

Finally a helicopter came, but again the

man shouted, 'I don't need you, Jesus is going to save me.'

Finally he could hold on no longer so he fell from the cliff and died.

When he got to Heaven he cornered Jesus and said, 'I thought you were going to save me.'

'Well,' said Jesus, 'I sent a boat, a submarine, and a helicopter ...'

Report from a school magazine about the annual nativity play:

'Though most of the parents had seen a nativity play before they still laughed loudly throughout.'

This fellow was desperately short of money and needed €100 very urgently. So he wrote a letter to Jesus begging for the money and addressed it simply to 'Jesus'.

It was opened at the post office and the staff there were so touched they took up a collection which came to €90. So they posted this to the fellow and waited for the reaction. Sure enough a few days later there was another letter addressed to Jesus. When they opened it, it read:

> *Dear Jesus,*
> *Thank you for the money. But next time don't send it through the mail because those thieving bastards at the post office stole €10 of it.*

Extract from a schoolboy's essay:

'I know Jesus loves everyone, but He never met my little sister.'

During the bad old days of apartheid a black man sat crying on the steps of a church in

South Africa. Jesus was walking along and asked him why he was weeping.

'They won't let me in, Lord,' he replied.

'I know exactly how you feel,' said Jesus, 'I haven't been able to get in there myself for years.'

Jesus would not have made a great funeral director. Every funeral he attended he broke up – including his own.

A recently converted Christian was asked if he believed that Jesus turned water into wine.

'I haven't got that far yet,' he replied, 'but in the short time I have known Him He has turned wine into groceries and children's clothes.'

What is the name of the dog Jesus mentions in the gospel?

Moreover. (Moreover, the dog came and licked his sores)

The children in school were asked to draw a nativity scene. One little boy had Jesus and Mary and Joseph in the stable and behind them was a big fat man.

'Who is that?' asked the teacher, pointing to the big fat man.

'That,' said the little boy, 'is Round John Virgin.'

A modern kid was saying his prayers before going to bed. His mother heard him finish the Lord's prayer with the words: 'And deliver us from email, Amen.'

If it had been three wise women who visited

Jesus in Bethlehem, how would things have been different?

Well, they would have asked for directions.

They would have arrived on time.

They would have helped deliver the baby.

They would have cleaned the stable.

They would have made a casserole.

And they would have brought disposable nappies as gifts.

*H*UMOUR IN THE BIBLE

Did Jesus Himself have a sense of humour? Is there humour in the Bible and the Gospels? These are deep and weighty questions about which whole books have been written and they must be at least mentioned even in a joke book like this.

If Jesus Christ was true man and true God then He must have laughed and seen the need for humour from time to time because humour is one of the few things common to all human beings. But humour takes many forms and manifests itself in many different ways in different cultures at different periods in history. Jokes for example, especially in the abstract form in which we use them today, are a relatively modern phenomenon. Jesus liked to tell parables, little stories He used to teach people and get His point across. These parables were not meant to be funny, but they often had the same structure as jokes and were easy to remember. Most importantly, they were understood and appreciated by their target audience.

In order to write this part of the book, I have re-read the Gospels in their entirety, an interesting experience which I would recommend to anyone. Let me list the episodes and incidents that struck me as humorous or that had humorous potential.

Saint Matthew's gospel begins with nearly forty 'begats' (one of whom was Booz) from Abraham right down to Joseph of the House of David. But Joseph was not the father of Jesus – just His foster father, so what is the point of all of this? Superficially, it could be just a joke, but in Jewish tradition, my clerical brother informs me, adopted sons were fully integrated into the family and became an integral part of the family line.

The story of Martha and Mary entertaining Jesus divides Christians into two camps. Martha was the do-er, the cook, the housewife, representing work and toil. Her sister Mary was the mediator, the one who prayed and sat listening to the words of Jesus while Martha slaved in the kitchen.

Was Jesus joking when He said, 'Mary has chosen the better part?' i.e. the softer life.

If the Pharisees had asked Him to choose between them, what would He have replied?

Perhaps one of the greatest lateral thinkers of all time, he would have smiled and said, 'I love them both equally – Martha before dinner and Mary after.'

Jesus founded His church on a pun – thou art Peter and upon this rock I will build my church. The word 'Peter' means rock (from which we get petrol).

Jesus often spoke in riddles and many of His sayings involved paradoxes and seeming contradictions. For example, He said, 'The first shall be last and the last first', and, 'Whosoever shall save his life let him lose it.'

When asked if it was lawful to give tribute to Caesar or not (a trick question where either a yes or no answer would get Him into trouble), He confounded His enemies with clever wordplay by replying, 'Render to Caesar the things that are Caesar's and to God the things that are God's.'

When asked if it was easy for a rich man to enter Heaven, Jesus replied that it was easier for a camel to pass through the eye of a needle. Certainly, He was being funny here because a camel can be interpreted as a thick rope while others say that there was a gateway in Jerusalem called the eye of a needle.

On one occasion the mother of James and John the sons of Zebedee asked Jesus if when He came into his kingdom one of her sons could sit on His right hand and the other on His left. He must have given a wry smile and thought to himself, 'Here I am trying to save mankind from its sins and all this broad is interested in is good positions for her two boys.' And riding into Jerusalem on a donkey on the feast of palms has to be a joke – a king on an ass is surely a taunt to all worldly leaders.

The parable of the wise virgins and the foolish virgins is just asking to be joked about and has been many times. An innocent preacher once remarked, 'My dear brethren, which would you prefer – to be in the light with the wise virgins, or in the dark with the foolish virgins?'

Like most of us, Jesus did not like being laughed at, and when He told the bystanders that the daughter of Jarius was not dead but sleeping, they laughed Him to scorn. But when He raised her from the dead the smile was on the other side of their faces.

The dishonest steward who was dismissed and gave discount to all his boss's clients was praised by Jesus for his astute actions. This just has to be a joke – no explanation is possible other than that Jesus is contradicting Himself. And when the tax collector of small stature, Zacchaeus, climbed a tree to see his lord, Jesus must have looked up and smiled at least. At the wedding feast of Cana, performing his first miracle, Jesus turned water into wine, and wine superior to what had already been served. This smacks of a good sense of humour.

In the famous journey to Emmaus, after Jesus' resurrection, one of His disciples Cleopas asked Him, 'Are you the only visitor to Jerusalem who does not know the things that have happened there recently?'

'What things?' asked Jesus and this question alone proves He liked to joke.

'Are you a king?' Pilate asked Him.

'You said it,' He replied.

Take the case of the woman accused of adultery. As her accusers one by one crept away realising their own sins, Jesus looked up at the woman and humorously said, 'Woman, where are they? Has no one condemned you?' And He asked the Samaritan woman at the well to go call her husband, knowing full well that she had had five husbands and was then living with a man who was not her husband. This is impish, even provocative humour.

The Apostles of Jesus claimed that He often spoke in riddles and not everyone understood Him. Humour is a very powerful educational tool and Jesus used it frequently to get His point across. Jesus was a joyful person who preached a joyful message – and humour is one of the ultimate expressions of joy. Many commentators would have us believe that humour and jokes belong to the realm of Satan – the theme of Umberto Eco's *The Name of a Rose* – but surely, this is a perverted view. Some of the holiest and best-living people I have encountered have also had a wicked sense of humour.

A PRAYER FOR TODAY:

Dear Jesus,
You should be proud of me so far today. I haven't gossiped or lost my temper or stolen anything; I haven't been greedy, nasty or self-ish or lusted after anything or anybody. Now in a few minutes I'm going to get out of bed and after that I'm probably going to need all the help you can send me. Amen.

This is a joke I first heard in primary school: If Jesus had given us a ninth beatitude, what would it have been?

Blessed is he who sits on a pin for he is sure to rise again.

Winter Christianity: Many are cold but few are frozen.

A Scottish preacher was preaching his favourite words of Jesus from the pulpit.

'And the sinners,' he thundered, 'will be cast into exterior darkness, where there will be weeping and gnashing of teeth.'

'What about me?' one elder shouted back, 'I've lost all my teeth years ago.'

'Teeth will be provided,' answered the preacher.

A well-known farmer was listening to a preacher telling the story of how the shepherds visited Jesus at Bethlehem.

'All I can say,' he commented, 'is that if those shepherds were working for me, I'd have sacked all of them.'

'Jesus can do everything,' said a teacher in a religion class.

'No teacher,' said little Johnny, 'there is one thing He cannot do.'

'And what is that?' asked the teacher.

'He cannot please everyone,' said little Johnny.

Apparently there were originally four Wise Men planning to visit the baby Jesus on the way to Bethlehem, but one of them said he knew a short-cut.

The elderly parish priest was conducting the Stations of the Cross for his congregation. When he was about halfway through the fourteen stations, the sacristan arrived and whispered in his ear that there was an urgent sick call to which he had to attend at once. So he said to the sacristan, 'You know these stations – continue the service and I'll be back in a moment.'

So he went to the house of the seriously ill parishioner and administered the last rites and, on being offered a glass of whiskey and a sandwich, he availed of the hospitality. After a long chat lasting over an hour he suddenly remembered the service he was conducting and rushed back to the church. He was just in time to hear the sacristan intone: 'The two hundred and forty seventh station, Jesus stabs Judas with a bread knife.'

Roses are reddish
Violets are bluish
If it wasn't for Jesus
We'd all be Jewish

In the film *King of Kings* the part of Mary was played by Irish actress Siobhán McKenna. One film critic suggested it should have been called *Jesus, Was Your Mother Born in Ireland?*

Jesus once gave Saint Peter a list of people who were not to be allowed into Heaven under any circumstances. Walking around Heaven one day He met several of them so He asked Saint Peter why His orders were not obeyed.

'Well,' said Saint Peter, 'I let none of them through the gates of Heaven but your mother opened a window and let them all in.'

A new Pope took over the Catholic Church and was told by his secretary that in the Vatican safe there was a letter from Jesus himself that had never been opened by any Pope and he hoped that the present Pope would continue this tradition. The Pope said he would but one night his curiosity got the better of him so he sneaked down to the safe, opened it and took out the letter. With trembling hands he opened the envelope and examined the letter. It was signed by Jesus all right but it turned out to be the bill for the last supper.

An Orangeman, and a Belfast Protestant to boot, was passing by a Catholic religious shop full of holy medals statues of saints, crucifixes and the like. So he picked up a stone and threw it through the window shouting, 'Jesus Christ, I cannot stand all this bigotry.'

A Franciscan, a Benedictine and a Jesuit were transported back in time to meet the Holy Family of Jesus, Mary and Joseph.

The Franciscan fell to his knees and began to pray.

The Benedictine realised he would need three extra bottles of wine.

The Jesuit said, 'That's a splendid little boy

you have there – no doubt you'll be sending him to Stonyhurst.'

A motorist bought a little statue of Jesus to have in his car to protect him from having an accident.

As he hung it up on the dashboard he happened to notice something written underneath. It said:

'The protective power of this statue runs out at sixty miles per hour.'

A woman, who was a very strong believer in Jesus, was about to go on an urgent journey when she locked her keys in her car. So she prayed to Jesus to send help and right enough the first man passing by was able to help her and open the car.

'Praise be to Jesus,' she shouted, 'for sending me such a nice man.'

'I am not a nice man lady,' he growled, 'I just got out of jail a few hours ago after doing ten years for car theft.'

'Praise be to Jesus,' said the woman, 'for sending me a professional.'

If Jesus were alive today (and many people believe He is) would He be handing out buttons with the slogan:

WHAT PART OF 'THOU SHALT NOT' DON'T YOU UNDERSTAND?

We live in an increasingly secular world. A woman went into a shop to buy an ornamental crucifix for her house. The shop assistant asked her, 'Do you want one with a little man on it?'

Three blondes arrived at the gates of Heaven and were told they could enter if they could answer one simple question. Saint Peter asked them, 'What is Easter?'

The first blonde said, 'It's a feast in November when we all eat Thanksgiving turkey,' so she wasn't allowed in.

The second blonde said, 'It's a celebration of the birth of Jesus when we all exchange presents', so she didn't get in either.

The third said, 'Easter is a Christian feast that coincides with the Jewish Passover. After the last supper Jesus was falsely convicted by the Romans and crucified. He was buried in a nearby cave which was sealed off by a large boulder. But a few days later He moved back the boulder and emerged alive from his tomb.'

'You can come into Heaven,' smiled Saint Peter.

'But,' continued the third blonde, 'when he saw his shadow, he decided there would be six more weeks of winter, so he went back into his tomb.'

The Archbishop of Canterbury was visiting Rome and decided to pay a courtesy call to the Pope at the Vatican. He was ushered into the Pope's inner sanctum and given afternoon tea and muffins. He noticed a white telephone by the Pope's side so he asked him what it was for.

'That's a direct line to Jesus,' said the Pope, 'go on, try it, it will only cost me one euro.'

'Well', said the Archbishop shyly, 'we have a red telephone in Lambeth Palace, which is also a direct line to Jesus, but we use it only very rarely because it costs ten thousand pounds for a call lasting just a minute.'

'But you must remember', smiled the Pope, 'here that is only a local call.'

A little girl was asked in religion class in school why Jesus in the Lord's Prayer had told us to ask for our daily bread.

'So we would have it fresh every day,' she replied.

A psychiatrist arrives at the gates of Heaven and is immediately ushered in by Saint Peter without the usual interrogation.
'Thank heavens you've come,' he said to the psychiatrist, 'we've got a real problem on our hands. Jesus thinks he's Bertie Ahern.'

Who is Jesus' favourite athlete?
Adam – because he came first in the human race.

We all know Eve came second and Lazarus came fourth – but who came third?

An old Irish priest went to Lourdes and was being searched at the airport on his way home. The customs official discovered six large bottles of a clear liquid in his suitcase.

'What's that?' asked the official.

'Just holy water from Lourdes,' said the priest.

The official opened one bottle and having sniffed it said, 'It smells more like vodka to me.'

'Jesus be praised,' said the priest, 'another miracle.'

There is a rumour circulating in the newspapers that the Pope has approved a new low-fat, gluten-free, low-cholesterol communion wafer. Wits have already dubbed it, 'I can't believe it's not Jesus.'

Jesus, a keen golfer, sneaked down to Earth to play a round of golf and asked Moses to accompany Him. On the first hole, Jesus played into the water hazard so Moses parted the water and retrieved the ball. On the next hole, Jesus again drove into the water, but Moses refused to retrieve it this time. So Jesus walked on the water and played the ball where it lay. The caddy said to Moses, 'Who does that guy think he is, Jesus Christ?'

'No,' said Moses, 'He thinks He's Tiger Woods.'

One weekend, a priest was visiting a psychiatric hospital when he saw a fellow sitting in the corner with a t-shirt which bore the message:

I AM JESUS.

So the priest went over to him and said just to humour him, 'Did you really perform the miracle of the loaves and the fishes?'

'Look,' said the fellow, 'today is Sunday, my day of rest, and I don't talk shop.'

A little boy was taking a religious exam. One of the questions was, 'As well as the shepherds, who visited the baby Jesus in the stable at Bethlehem?'
He thought for a moment and wrote:
'The three Wise Guys.'

At a religious class, a little girl was asked what she knew about Good Friday. 'He was the fellow,' she said, 'who did all the work for Robinson Crusoe.'

'Is Jesus everywhere?' a curious child asked her father.
'Yes love,' he smiled at her.

'Is Jesus in my friend Shirley's back garden?' she persisted.

'Yes love,' smiled the indulgent father, 'Jesus is in your friend Shirley's back garden.'

'That's funny,' said the child, 'because my friend Shirley doesn't have a back garden.'

A little boy told his mother, 'We had a hymn in school today about a poor animal that couldn't see very well.'

'I don't recall that hymn,' said the worried mother, 'what was it called?'

'Gladly, the cross-eyed bear,' said the little boy.

A poor golfer who loves the game passionately prays to Jesus that there will be golf courses in Heaven and that he will score a hole-in-one there. Jesus answers his prayers with good news, better news and bad news.

Good news: There are golf courses in Heaven.
Better news: You will get a hole-in-one there.
Bad news: You are due to tee-off tomorrow morning at 9:30 a.m.

Why are there so many Jesus golf jokes? Here is yet another:

A famous golfer was at the gates of Heaven being given his final judgement by Jesus himself. 'I'm afraid I took your name in vain Lord during a golf match,' he confessed.

'Tell me the circumstances, my son,' said Jesus.

'Well,' said the golfer, 'I was on the final tee of a major tournament needing only a par five to win, when I drove my ball into the deep rough.'

'Was that when you took my name in vain?' asked Jesus.

'No Lord, I drove the ball up the fairway, but it landed in a fairway bunker.'

'And was that when you took my name in vain?' asked Jesus.

'No Lord, I blasted out of the fairway bunker but straight into a greenside bunker.'

'And was that when you took my name in vain, my son?' asked Jesus.

'No Lord,' said the golfer, 'I played a superb recovery to within a foot of the hole.'

'Ah God Almighty, don't tell me you missed the bloody putt!' said Jesus.

*T*HREE REASONS WHY

JESUS MIGHT HAVE BEEN BLACK

1. He called everyone Brother
2. He liked Gospel
3. He couldn't get a fair trial

JESUS MIGHT HAVE BEEN IRISH

1. He lived with His parents until He was thirty
2. He believed His mother was a virgin
3. His mother believed He was God

JESUS MIGHT HAVE BEEN CALIFORNIAN:

1. He had long hair
2. He was always in sandals or barefoot
3. He founded a new religion

JESUS MIGHT HAVE BEEN ITALIAN:

1. He moved His hands about when He talked
2. He had wine with every meal
3. He used olive oil all the time

JESUS MIGHT HAVE BEEN MEXICAN:

1. He had a Mexican name
2. He never had a steady job
3. He loved telling stories

JESUS MIGHT HAVE BEEN A WOMAN:

1. He had to feed a crowd of five thousand at a moments notice when there was very little food
2. He kept trying to get a message across to a bunch of men who just didn't get it
3. Even when He was dead He had to get up because there was more for Him to do

To conclude I wish to share with you one of my favourite jokes involving the words of Jesus:

A top executive of Coca Cola went to the Pope and offered him a quarter of a million euro to change the words of the Lord's Prayer to, 'Give us this day our daily coke.'

'I'm sorry,' said the Pope, 'the money would be welcome but I cannot change the words of Jesus as quoted in the bible.'

The executive comes back a week later.

'Your Holiness,' he announces, 'I have been authorised to increase my offer to half a million euro.'

'Sorry,' said the Pope, 'the answer is still no.'

Finally the executive offers one million euro and the Pope says, 'It is not in my power to do what you ask – I cannot discuss this any further.'

As he is leaving the Vatican the executive says to his PA, 'I wonder how much the bread people are paying him?'